OUTDOOR SKETCHING

CREATIVE ARTS LIBRARY

Other Titles in Preparation

OUTDOOR SKETCHING

Presenting

SOME FUNDAMENTAL PRINCIPLES FOR
THE GUIDANCE OF STUDENTS OF OUTDOOR
SKETCHING AND PICTURE MAKING

by

Ernest W. Watson

WATSON-GUPTILL

PUBLICATIONS, INC.

NEW YORK

1 9 4 6

To my WIFE
Artist Companion
on many a
Sketching
Trip

Gallery of Examples

JUMBLED BUILDINGS

COLOR DRAWING WITH BRUSH AND PEN BY THE AUTHOR

The original (6¾ x 9¼ inches) was made directly from nature. The washes were applied first in the lightest tones; darker values were added over the first washes as may be seen in the shadow areas of the building and the foliage. A very limited palette was employed. The ink lines were made last, to accent the drawing and to suggest details.

OUTDOOR SKETCHING

OUTDOOR sketching is one of the most rewarding experiences in the life of an artist. Whether one is learning the first steps or has achieved a measure of mastery, sketching is an altogether delightful pastime. For my part, I can say that my pleasantest memories are of sketching adventures with pencil and brush, both at home and abroad. And every sketch seen a year or ten years later brings back the sight and the feel of all the interesting things that happened on the day it was made.

In spite of the joys that are in store for the sketcher, his first meetings with nature are likely to be a bit awkward — perhaps discouraging. Unskilled in the handling of his medium, he lacks·the language needed to record the things nature says to him and the response he would make if he possessed the power. His position is not unlike that of a man who finds himself in a foreign land where he can neither understand the unknown tongue nor make his own thoughts articulate. Thus he has two problems: learning a language and making an acquaintance.

It might be thought that mastery of the "language," that is, technical skill, is the whole story. If one can say what he desires, graphically, can he not see plainly what is before him in a landscape and record it with his newly-won skill? The answer, of course, is *no*. Nature is complex, at times mysterious, full of contradictions, full of surprises. Her aspects vary with the seasons; her moods change with the coming of storms and fog. She is full of subtleties which only the artist can discover by being a persistent and studious suitor. Painters spend a lifetime in their search for greater intimacy.

Is the prospect, then, disheartening? It might well be so for the weakly intentioned; for those in whom the fire of desire burns brightly the quest is full of high adventure, rewarding at every step along the way. The enlargement of one's power of expression and the awareness of new beauties in nature are great sources of delight. We are surprised, as we draw or paint, to discover that we are developing a sort of sixth sense that lets us into secrets reserved for the artist's penetrating search. What this amounts to is the fact that we never really see things until we feel them, as it were, with pencil or brush — our sixth sense.

Learning a graphic language is, as I have said, a somewhat awkward performance, whatever the medium might be. And the student of outdoor sketching is well advised to start in the simplest possible way. Do not begin with color. I realize that others may disagree with this admonition, but it seems reasonable not to impose the problems of full color representation at the outset. There is so much that can be learned through black and white mediums which, indeed, constitute the entire careers of many artists in the graphic arts field. And so in this book we devote ourselves almost exclusively to sketching in pencil, pen, charcoal, and wash. The chapter on color drawings and the color plates are included to suggest the natural transition from black and white to color.

The equipment required by the black and white mediums is simple and inexpensive: a portfolio for drawing papers and a small flat box, that slips in one's pocket, to hold pencils or charcoal. The portfolio serves as a drawing board. Two large rubber bands can be used to hold the papers securely to the portfolio while drawing. A folding campstool is indispensable. Light metal stools which fold up to about 8 x 15 inches will serve very well. They are easily carried under the arm with the portfolio. Nor should one forget a good thick newspaper. There are occasions when a stone wall, a grassy bank or a fallen log happen to be desirable vantage points from which to view the subject. The newspaper serves as a cushion and as protection from cold and dampness.

I have referred to the great variety of nature's appearances under different weather conditions. The student will soon learn which of these favors his subjects and makes his work most interesting. The experienced sketcher is not likely to prefer high noon to either early morning or later afternoon, when long shadows are cast by a low sun on fields and streets. These not only lend dramatic design patterns to the scene; they reveal forms of trees, landscapes, and buildings with their clearly defined shadow patterns.

It is a most rewarding exercise to make studies of the same subject at different times throughout the day. I recall seeing about a dozen sketches in watercolor made by a prominent illustrator. They were studies of his own country home seen under the changing conditions of light, hour by hour, on a sunny day.

Every artist has had the experience of being surprised at the beauty of some familiar spot which had never before been dramatized — for him — by the unusual condition which finally arrested his attention. Sometimes it is fog which reduces complex forms to simple silhouettes; it may be the floodlight of a lightning flash, or the violent rush of wind that often precedes a midsummer thunder shower.

A most annoying experience to students who go forth in search of good sketching subjects is to return home without having found one. This kind of fruitless adventure is not unknown even to the professional artist. Once, when in the studio of a well-known New York painter, I was admiring a recent canvas. It was a picture of rolling hills in the Pennsylvania countryside. The artist chuckled: "That picture is a sort of accident; it was done late one afternoon of a day unsuccessfully spent in looking for a subject that would interest me. Had it not been for a blow-out which occurred on top of the hill overlooking the scene represented on that canvas, I would have returned home without a sketch. Getting out of my car, I took a look around before starting to put on the spare. 'Look at that,' I exclaimed to my wife, indicating the landscape, 'I've got to paint that before bothering with tires.' "

When visiting exhibitions it is revealing to note the many paintings of subjects which most of us would pass by as unworthy of even a quick sketch. In this connection I recall noting a fine painting, by Edward Hopper, of a railroad crossing in a flat, scrubby pine landscape which would certainly not impress one as promising picture material. The moral is that we must not expect too much of nature. Sometimes, to be sure, she will present us with a finished picture; more often it will be only the makings of a picture.

Many sketches brought in from the field will be set down as failures — and no doubt they will be. But do not tear them up. It is encouraging as one progresses to look back upon past efforts, the better to appreciate what progress has been made. Now and then, too, in examining our "failures" we are surprised to come upon one that really looks good, so good that we wonder how we could have put it with the discards. The reason for this is simple. On the day when that particular drawing was made we were trying for a very special effect which we failed to capture. Our disappointment blinded us to other excellent qualities which were unconsciously achieved, though not recognized at the time. Because our original purpose was not accomplished we could see no good at all in the work. Several years ago I made a sketch on the back of a color drawing that had been discarded. I liked the new sketch and put it into a frame. While planning this book I decided to reproduce it on these pages. When I took it from the frame I discovered the forgotten color drawing on the back. That long lost drawing was "Jumbled Buildings" which you now see as the frontispiece.

The sketching student will do well to study etchings, lithographs, and prints of all kinds. These, to be sure, are something more than sketches. But for that reason they are all the more instructive. They have been carefully studied for all those qualities one would like to achieve in an outdoor sketch. Working from these prints directly, translating them into whatever medium one is using at the time, is an excellent exercise for inclement weather when outside work is impractical.

The *Gallery of Examples* from the work of other artists, which occupies the latter part of this book, constitutes a valuable addition to the instruction offered in the earlier pages. These plates represent a great variety of approach and treatment. Those by Roy Brown and Henry Varnum Poor were done as preliminary studies for paintings. Two or three, I believe, were made as book illustrations; all, I am sure, were done outdoors. They deserve careful study.

Some artists who love to sketch outdoors are greatly restricted in their work by timidity — by the fear of attention from passers-by. This is a great pity, because so many fascinating subjects can only be sketched by working in places where people are able to peer over one's shoulder. This is disconcerting at first but one can get used to it. Artists are seldom actually interfered with: they are usually greatly respected. Small boys may crowd uncomfortably around, but they are easily managed. An older one will likely enough assume protective authority and keep the rest at a comfortable distance. If one's campstool should fall into a Venetian canal one of the lads will take off his clothes and go after it as an Italian kid did after mine.

In going through my portfolios to assemble material for this book, I based my selection of drawings and instructional content upon the assumption that readers would represent a wide range of ability, training, experience and interest. Some I pictured as beginners who might hope to find guidance in their very first graphic adventures; others, having successfully taken the first steps, would be looking for fresh worlds to conquer; some, already highly proficient with brush and pencil, would be interested in whatever new slants might be seen in a fellow artist's work.

Such, I envisioned and hoped, would be my audience, and I desired that my book would have something worth while for all. Obviously, then, it could not be planned in the manner of a textbook, which presupposes a given background in a particular student group, and proceeds in a series of progressive lessons to instruct such students in the way the author thinks they should go. Except for some sequentially planned lessons in the first pages, which do develop an idea that I consider quite fundamental, the book is a rather miscellaneous collection of drawings and suggestions that I trust will prove to be worthy of study.

In view of this approach the instruction to be gleaned on these pages is as casual as it would be if the reader had spent a few weeks with me and accompanied me on many a sketching trip. In such an event the hows and why would be suggested by the kind of things that were done from day to day, rather than by a premeditated course of study. It is a fortuitous rather than an academically planned procedure, and I consider it to be more fruitful. This way it is more fun for both pupil and master, and if sketching is not fun there is no point in becoming interested in it.

In sketching, as in any form of pictorial expression, the artist is confronted with three basic problems:

1. Legibility — First he has to learn how to make a reasonable facsimile of the object he sets out to represent. This implies some knowledge of perspective, a sense of proportion, and an understanding of how light, with resulting shadows, creates impressions of form. He has to be aware of these things and be able to express them to make his drawing or painting legible.

2. Composition — Whenever we put two spots down on paper or canvas we create a problem in composition — or design, which is the same thing. The second spot — whether it be a man, a horse, a boat, a tree, or even a cloud — is put down in the place where it is considered most effective in relation to the first object or mass. Every added stroke of pencil or brush is controlled by this consideration of design. Sometimes, though rarely, our subject is so agreeably arranged by nature that it satisfies our sense of design and can be transcribed to paper or canvas with little compositional change. Usually the picture the artist brings home is far from a camera likeness of the scene that he is depicting. He is an expert scene-shifter, moving mountains, trees and buildings about at will in order to achieve a well-organized design. This, of course, is the creative faculty at work. The exercise of that faculty is the final reward for artist or amateur who at first may find complete contentment in merely reproducing what he sees before him.

3. Rendering — There remains the problem of rendering. This is a technical problem that few artists, even the very skillful, feel is ever finally solved. It confronts the beginner in his very first efforts. He is puzzled as to how to set down his pencil lines and how to manage his brush strokes. In planning this book, I asked myself to what extent I ought to discuss rendering problems: the techniques of pencil, pen, and brush. If I were to attempt much in this direction, I concluded, I would certainly have little paper left for the things I most wanted to present. No book, unless of an encyclopedic character, can tell the whole story. As a matter of fact, the drawings by twenty-six artists here shown do demonstrate a very wide range of technical performance. There are excellent books on pencil, pen, watercolor, pastel, and oil painting which the student will doubtless wish to add to his library of technical instruction as his increasing skill demands greater scope for expression.

All of these comments relate to what might be termed "finished" sketches. Painters make innumerable sketches that are nothing more than diagrams which, though valuable as notes to aid memory, are not intended to be seen by others for whom they would have no meaning.

Some of the pages in this book may be familiar to readers of *American Artist*, because I have included considerable material which has appeared in that magazine during the past several years, particularly drawings by other artists in the *Gallery of Examples*.

The chief virtue of an instruction book, as of a personal teacher, is its inspiration for the student. The exact nature of the instruction is of less importance if the reader is stimulated to take up his pencil, pen or brush and pursue his experiments with enthusiasm and persistence.

A PEN SKETCH BY CONSTANTIN GUYS (1805–1892)

ON THE SPOT PENCIL SKETCH, MADE BY THE AUTHOR
AT THE TIME HE TOOK THE PHOTOGRAPH OPPOSITE

This drawing, slightly larger than the halftone reproduction above, was done with a very soft graphite pencil. The paper, though not rough, is by no means smooth, the combination of soft lead and roughish paper giving an effect somewhat suggestive of charcoal.

4

It is summer in the country. The young artist with his campstool and portfolio steps from the road to find just the right view of the weathered old barn.

As he stands there surveying the scene, he is doubtless forming a mental picture of the effect he hopes to create with his pencil or brush. He is striving to get a preview of it. What really does he see, and what will his sketch look like? Would another artist standing beside him see the same thing, and would his painting be like his neighbor's? We know of course that the scene would impress each artist differently and that the two sketches would be remarkably unlike, even though each artist were reasonably faithful to the facts before him.

This is because the scene filters through the personality and temperament of the artist before it emerges in graphic form on paper or canvas. Imagination plays upon it, mood colors it. The picture will be an interpretation rather than stark reality, that is, if the painter is really an artist. It will have a feeling, a quality, not to be discovered in the scene by any other person. Thus it is that pictures by great artists shine with "the light that never was on sea or land." Thus it is that a Corot landscape is a poem in color more than it is a paint-

ing of a particular scene in the French countryside.

This creative aspect of art is of course its very essence, and is wholly beyond the reach of the teacher to impart. One either has it or has it not. Let us acknowledge that the essence of a work of art cannot be laid bare by cold analysis, that there is much in the creation of a picture which defies dissection and exposition; we can nevertheless teach something of the grammar and anatomy of art expression. We can lead the student quickly through experiments in various graphic ways and means which he must master before he is able to function as an artist.

But let us get back to our young friend by the roadside and see what kind of problem lies before him. With whatever mood or feeling he may wish to invest his study of the barn, he must express himself in the language of form, a language based upon simple and fundamental facts of appearance. He must learn this language thoroughly at the outset, just as a writer and a musician have to school themselves as beginners in the precepts which underlie their particular arts.

First of all a picture ought to be legible — that is, clearly defined and understandable. The forms, whether of buildings, foliage or figures, must look like

the objects which they are intended to represent. Form is made manifest by three kinds of visual impressions: by silhouette — the shape of its bulk against the sky or other background — by light and shadow, and by color. So far as our present discussion is concerned we can forget color. That will simplify the lesson to be learned. But we can not dispense with either silhouette or light and shadow.

All objects have both silhouette, and light and shadow. In some silhouette is predominant, in others light and shadow. The first impression of our barn is its dark bulk patterned against the sky. In sketch 1 we have brushed-in its silhouette with a perfectly flat wash to emphasize this phase of the effect.

It is evident that the light and shadow element not only is needed here to express the facts of form, but that it is the aspect of our subject that we are going to rely upon chiefly to supply illustrative content and pattern interest. In sketch 2 we dramatize this aspect by indicating all shaded parts and cast shadows with a uniform black ink wash, leaving the lighted areas white.

By combining the pictorial aspects of sketches 1 and 2, we have sketch 3 which is a close approximation of the subject as seen in the photograph, except for the light shed roof. This simple demonstration convinces us that the general appearance of objects can frequently be got by very limited means and it should encourage the student, in all his work, to try to grasp first the big significant form facts before his interest fastens upon incidental details.

How clearly such drawings reveal the basic structure of objects! As a first step preparatory to outdoor sketching no exercise could be more profitable than the making of innumerable ink drawings of this sort. They teach how to interpret the subject in a bold dramatic manner. They demonstrate that the subtle and detailed effects which often hypnotize the beginner are not essential — such effects, for example, as the slight differences of tone on the weathered boards. These drawings lead the student to see his subject as a unit rather than a conglomeration of details and they prevent his becoming confused by tone and color complications when he goes outdoors to paint.

Another thing — these studies in black and white reveal the part played by pattern in picture-making. Indeed it is impossible to exaggerate the value of this work done with a No. 3 sable brush and a bottle of india ink.

Turning the pages of this book the reader may think that an inordinate amount of attention is being given this kind of approach to his sketching instruction. But after many years of teaching the subject to hundreds of students, I do not hesitate to say that this simple analytical introduction to outdoor sketching is about the most valuable contribution I have been able to make. It is surprising how persistently students have to be reminded of this A B C of graphic representation; to be brought back to these fundamentals of silhouette and shadow pattern, even after they appear to have learned the lesson through repeated exercises such as are presented on these pages.

Now for further experiments with our barn. In sketch 4 the barn roof and that of the shed are left white. Not only has the drawing acquired sparkle and

1

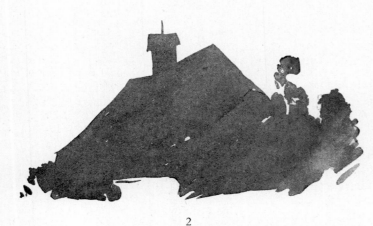

2

3

6

pattern interest: it is more legible because it shows the roof receiving more light than does the side, as in the photograph.

Coming to sketch 5, we note that a light patch of tone has been brushed over the far end of the roof to lend a sense of mass to the structure. The darkening of the cupola also contributes to this result. Thus we have secured the effect of silhouette by merely suggesting it.

We have added another compositional element in this sketch: that is *tone gradation*. It is seen on the end of the barn. Gradation is very effective in creating dramatic composition, but the beginner should exercise care in using it because there is danger of interference with legibility.

This danger is suggested in sketch 6, where the tone gradation has been reversed, the darkest value being at the lower left corner. If this area were made *too* dark there would be little or no contrast with the deeply shaded front. For the sake of legibility we want to retain considerable contrast in this study, though we do not mean to suggest that it would be an artistic sin to let the dark on the end of the barn merge with the shaded front. Indeed there are many situations where it is undesirable to insist upon maximum legibility at every point in the picture. However, as legibility is the chief object of this lesson, we are seeking every means to emphasize it.

Sketch 6 presents another suggestion for silhouetting the roof, dark clouds bringing out its contour effectively.

Now let us turn to my own sketch of this farm scene, on page 4, made on the spot at the time I took the photograph. It shows, I think, how the kind of analysis we have been discussing is applied in a drawing made from nature.

First observe that, although many liberties have been taken with the subject (as reproduced in the photograph), the rendering is clearly based upon the approach seen in our diagrams. The shadow patterns have been kept simple — though not perfectly flat as in the brush drawings — and the silhouette aspect has been exploited.

The great elm is treated principally as silhouette, although it is full of tonal variation. Elm trees present less definite light and shade effects than maples, oaks, or other trees having denser foliage.

It will be noted that the bushes at the right have been given shapes quite unlike those in the photograph. In the wash drawings they have been treated in strong light and shadow and have been designed differently than those in the pencil sketch which are virtually silhouettes. In the latter, observe the way in which the bare tree trunk curves inward to carry the eye into the line of the cloud mass. It forms one end of an ellipse within which the entire composition is roughly enclosed. The small tree silhouette at the extreme left is so shaped as to complete the ellipse at that side of the picture. By changing the direction of the road, the sweep of the elliptical movement is completed at the bottom.

While it is not the intention to dwell upon rendering at this point, it might be pointed out that the handling of the pencil in this drawing is in the manner of that described on page 35. The pencil was of a soft grade, about 3B, and it was used with a rather dull point.

Since the surface of the paper had a slight "tooth," the tone assumes a slightly granular quality somewhat suggestive of charcoal. In a few places the tortillon stump was rubbed over the tones lightly to give them a smoother quality. This is especially clear on the grass in front of the barn, on the roof, and in places on the tree mass.

Pencil rendering with a single soft lead is recommended for first experiments in this medium. The method does not involve the technical difficulties encountered when several degrees of lead are employed and one gets into the problems discussed on page 34.

4

5

6

7

Sketching On a Gray Day

The subject of our experiments on the preceding pages was very simple because, seen in bright sunlight, the building presented clearly defined lighted and shaded planes, a ready-made tonal pattern.

Now let us see what we can do with a subject that, unlike the barn of our first study, stands out stark and gray — at first glance a very unpromising model, having a severe, unbroken silhouette and an almost uniformly gray tone covering all its planes. There is scarcely more than a hint of light and shadow.

Well, it is our privilege to imagine what the sun would do to the barn if it should suddenly break through the clouds. This we visualize in sketch 1, the light and shadow giving pattern interest and providing maximum legibility.

In an effort to add some silhouette interest we encourage a tree to grow up behind the structure and we move a telephone pole close to it on the right.

In sketch 2 we substitute the skeleton of a dead tree for the one in full foliage and try for better pattern effect in the foreground. In this the photograph has nothing to help us; we just have to create shapes that compose well.

Experiments in all these sketching exercises in brush and ink are facilitated if done on tracing paper laid over the first drawing, thus obviating the necessity of making new drawings for successive designs.

In sketches 3, 4, and 5 we continue our studies with the brush, and on the following page we carry the subject further with our pencil.

In sketch 3 we observe what can be added to the picture by the employment of a single gray tone with the black. We achieve better legibility because we differentiate between the roof plane of the lean-to and the gable end of the barn. It

SKETCH 1

SKETCH 2

helps also to represent the ground by the use of a lighter tone.

In sketch 4 we still confine ourselves to black and one uniform gray tone, but try a different placing of the gray. The darkened gable gives the building a better sense of mass, providing a more solid silhouette against the sky.

Now in sketch 5 we become more faithful to the subject by substituting dark gray for all shadows and confining the blacks to openings and to the foliage.

In sketch 6, the pencil sketch on the next page, I have tried quite exactly to follow the brush-drawn diagram of sketch 5. But the pencil has added its technical charm. When the subject is rendered at larger size, as it is in sketch 7, it is possible, even essential, to make it more illustrative by rendering detail and paying some attention to textures. We can afford to think of individual boards and allow ourselves some freedom in tonal variations within each plane. But we shall do well to keep those first simple diagrams in mind if we are tempted to monkey around too much within each plane area. I must ask myself, for example, if in trying to give textural expression to the roof of that lean-to I have broken up the plane too much; and if in trying to make the gable end more interesting I'm in error there. I'll leave it to you to decide.

The beginner is apt to be impatient with such exercises as those brush studies which precede a final rendering. He likes to finish before he begins. But once he starts brush experiments he will become fascinated with the illustrative possibilities of black and white and one or two additional tones. He must be sure to keep the tones flat; if they are permitted to get spotty the value of the exercise is entirely lost.

It is interesting to contrast the technique of the pencil drawings on page 10 with that of the one on page 4. The work on page 10 was rendered with three pencils of varying degrees (B, 2B, and 3B) on a rather smooth paper. The other drawing represents the effect of using a single soft pencil on a rough-surfaced paper.

The contrast of these two techniques will be noted in many drawings on following pages. Those on pages 34 and 35 present the same subject treated in both manners. The single soft pencil technique is certainly simpler for the beginner; it permits him to build up his tones cautiously — to feel his way, as it were.

Later on I shall have something to say about *size* in pencil drawing, but at this point I would like to caution the student not to make his pencil sketches large. The original drawing for sketch 7 is the exact size of the reproduction. The pencil is a *point* medium and it is at a disadvantage on a large scale, certainly when in the beginner's hand. It is easier, in a small sketch, to hold the composition under control, to keep it unified and comprehensive. A small sketch takes less time, a factor of some importance when working outdoors under difficult conditions.

SKETCH 3

SKETCH 4

SKETCH 5

9

SKETCH 6

SKETCH 7

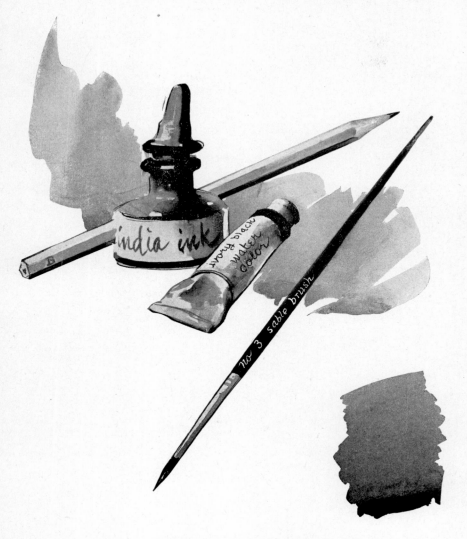

PENCIL

WATERPROOF
INDIA INK

IVORY BLACK
WATERCOLOR

SABLE BRUSH

How to Make Wash Drawings

Here is all you need for exercises in ink and wash shown on the preceding pages. Waterproof india ink is recommended for the black areas because it is not affected by the gray watercolor washes when they are brought up to, and touch, the edges of the black. Furthermore the ink assures a flat, even black which is important in these studies.

In laying gray washes the paper should be on an inclined drawing board and the brush should be full almost to the point of dripping. The wash will then "puddle" as shown in the illustration above. The puddle, traveling down the incline as you proceed to lay the wash, leaves a uniform tone of gray. The brush should be kept full by constant dipping so that the puddle is maintained. It should not be allowed to dry in the middle of the wash. When you get to the bottom, dry the brush and let it pick up the puddle. Enough of

the gray mixture should be prepared in a dish or palette to serve for all areas to be covered. The mixture should be stirred whenever the brush is dipped in order to keep it from settling.

The kind of paper is a factor too. You may want to try several surfaces before you decide which is best for this purpose. Most good quality pencil papers are suitable. Illustration boards are good too, but more expensive than necessary for these exercises.

It is important to make the washes as nearly flat and even in tone as possible. If they are allowed to become spotty they will not serve the purpose for which they are here recommended.

Best results will be obtained in small studies. The originals of all wash drawings shown on preceding pages are the exact size of the reproductions.

A good quality sable brush is needed for best results.

OLD FARMHOUSE　　　HALFTONE REPRODUCTION OF A WATERCOLOR BY THE AUTHOR

The two sketches on these facing pages show an application of the simple light and shade treatment to which the reader has been introduced in what has gone before. The pencil sketch was preceded by the watercolor that was done on the spot and is quite a literal transcription of the subject. The watercolor is small, not over 8 x 10 inches. That accounts for the utter simplicity of the sunlit areas, all of which were left white. Had the study been larger, doubtless it would have been desirable to indicate the detail, textures and color variation in those planes. I have discussed this relationship of detail to size of sketch on page 30. In this small sketch I thought the sparkle of pure white, cut out sharply from the surrounding color, was likely to be the most interesting effect I could produce. Indeed, in the brilliant sunshine of a clear summer morning the impression was not so different from my rendering as one might imagine. But that is neither here nor there; the only question is whether or not the result has spirit and charm. The sooner one loses the beginner's sense of obligation of being uncompromisingly faithful to his subject the greater will be his progress. What the artist tries to do is seize upon and dramatize the qualities that attract him. He is creator, not reporter.

The shaded sides of the buildings appear — in this halftone reproduction of the watercolor — to be quite uniform washes of color. In the original there is considerable variation of hue which of course is not revealed in the print. Color variation does not interfere with the desired simplicity of shadow planes so long as the values of different hues are kept relatively uniform.

The pencil study, done after returning to the studio, shows my preoccupation with simple light and shadow pattern, but the composition of the sketch has been radically altered. For one thing it had to be more elongated to serve a definite purpose — it was used in *American Artist* as a heading.

This drawing, by the way, was done on *Cameo* paper, a sheet which was obtainable before the war and which, I hope, will eventually be on the market again. Made for the printing of fine halftones, it was discovered by artists to be an unusual paper for drawings. It is coated with a clay preparation that has a "tooth" which is peculiarly receptive to the lead pencil. The clay coating is very heavy and it can be scraped away with a sharp knife or razor blade. Such otherwise difficult effects as small white spots surrounded by pencil tone can be secured simply by scraping them out of the dark mass with the blade. The wash on the line and other white accents were thus obtained in this sketch.

14

FISHERMEN'S COTTAGES SKETCHED BY THE AUTHOR, IN MOUSEHOLE, ENGLAND

Courtesy Joseph Dixon Crucible Co.

This pencil sketch of fishermen's cottages in the quaint little harbor of Mousehole in Cornwall, England, is one of many drawings I created as advertisements for the Eldorado pencil. The pattern diagram, opposite, appeared on the page with the completed sketch in order to demonstrate the very approach we have been discussing on these pages.

It is shown here to introduce a new element. In the diagram — as in the drawing — the shadow on the houses is rendered in a tone that gradually gets lighter as distance increases. This is, of course, a very elementary fact of perspective appearance, but it is worth noting here, where it is so clearly demonstrated in a subject made up largely of receding planes.

I find these diagrammatic analyses very instructive. They help to resolve the pictorial problem into its simplest and most dramatic aspect. They focus attention upon design and lead to greater pattern interest. Not that I often actually make such diagrams before proceeding with a sketch; the fact that I've done them innumerable times in teaching has made me pattern-conscious always. As I study my subject I "see" the pattern diagram overlayed upon the scene before me.

The rendering of this subject was done with leads of varying degrees of hardness. A very soft lead was employed for the darks of open doorways and all other blacks. An H pencil — very hard — sufficed for the lightest tones, as on the roof and end wall of the nearest building. Intermediate grades served for middle tones. Of course, it is always desirable to get along with as few leads as possible but it will be found that in this technique in which the pencils, sharpened as directed on page 34, are applied with considerable pressure, several leads are needed to produce tones that are pleasantly smooth.

The student might find it interesting to render this subject as it would appear if the sun were in a position to reverse the light and shadow effect. Then experiment with a clouded sky, suggestions for which will be found in various sketches throughout the book. Try, if you wish, such a rendering as that by Louis Rosenberg on page 57, or other techniques seen in the work of the many artists represented. The same suggestion for experimentation with different techniques might apply to most of the subjects in this book — good practice for indoor sketching during inclement weather.

15

16

PEN SKETCH BY THE AUTHOR

This pen drawing of an old blacksmith shop, together with the little pencil sketches on the page opposite, suggests how almost any subject may offer a variety of design possibilities. Before making a pen drawing I almost invariably try out compositions with my pencil at very small scale. These consume but little time and when an acceptable scheme is produced I can take up my pen with more confidence.

In a miniature study, detail can almost entirely be ignored and effort focused upon big compositional effects. This is true with almost every medium, but is especially so with pencil and pen. Thumbnail sketches like the smallest one opposite often suffice to crystallize one's idea sufficiently to serve as a safe guide for the larger and final drawing.

I do not think it will be disputed when I say that of all mediums the pen is about the least cooperative, hence one of the most difficult of tools in the hands of a beginner. It will only do what it is *forced* to do. Unlike other mediums — charcoal, for example — it will not give surprise effects, which, if one is clever, one can turn to pretty good advantage.

The *finality* of a pen stroke is another obstacle; once set down it is there to stay unless removed by very laborious erasure. Some day a manufacturer will produce a pen paper that eliminates this handicap. I can tell him how to make it, for I myself have created a surface that permits easy erasure by scraping with a razor blade — and without leaving a rough surface for further rendering. This is nothing more than tracing paper mounted on white cardboard. Wet the

tracing paper until saturated. With a bristle brush spread photo-mounting paste evenly over one side and paste the paper down on the board. Lacking a press of some sort, press the paper down by hand rubbing and then put it in a makeshift press of books or any heavy weight. The weight must be great — say fifty pounds. Unless the mounting board is unusually heavy, it is necessary to mount another piece of tracing paper similarly on the reverse side to prevent warping.

When it is dry, you have a sheet that takes india ink beautifully. You can blaze away on it with pen or brush, knowing that a gentle scrape of the razor blade (a new rather than a used one) will easily remove a tree, a horse or an elephant, leaving the erased area smooth and receptive to more ink. If you have been gentle in scraping, you can even make a second correction at the same point.

The best way to answer the question as to the kind of pens to use is to experiment with many different points from crow quills to stubs. Each person has his individual preferences which can only be determined by trial. Generally speaking, a pen which gives medium heavy lines is better than the delicate crow quill which can lead to fussiness and overelaboration.

Direction of pen strokes is always puzzling to the novice. Constant study of drawings by professional illustrators will be helpful. These will be found in children's books, many of which are illustrated in black and white.

As an exercise in rendering, it would be profitable to make pen renderings of the pencil sketches on page 16.

COAL SHEDS ON THE WATERFRONT   PHOTO BY THE AUTHOR

I took this photograph of some old coal sheds on Wallabout Canal in Brooklyn after I had made the pencil drawing on page 19, because I thought the subject excellent for the discussion of procedure in developing a focal point of interest in a vignetted sketch. The sketches on page 20 are intended to illustrate the *thought* process that led up to the pencil drawing.

First, I was impressed by the beauty of the shadow pattern. This is expressed in sketch 1, which interprets the pattern in a single flat tone of gray. It was interest in this pattern that induced me to make the sketch.

The second sketch represents my plan to create a focus of interest near the center by means of very dark values at this point, lightening the tones at both sides.

The third sketch shows how I visualized further development of the picture by the addition of other tones.

The slanting gray mass across the face of the pier has no counterpart in the photograph. It seemed desirable thus to break across that white horizontal space and make a connection between water and the level above.

The pencil drawing itself was done on a fairly smooth sheet of paper with several degrees of leads. The blacks were produced by a 4B, the intermediate grays with 3B and 2B, and the lightest tones with HB. The degree of leads required for various tones depends a good deal upon the weather. On damp, humid days paper absorbs much moisture and much softer leads are needed than on dry days. It is advisable to have at hand plenty of pencils of all degrees.

The drawing is 7 x 11 inches. I seldom make sketches larger than this. To do so takes an inordinate amount of time and nothing seems to be gained.

PENCIL SKETCH BY THE AUTHOR

SKETCH 1

SKETCH 2

 SKETCH 3

Paper

"Paper is part of the picture." This truism, adopted by an American manufacturer of drawing papers as an advertising slogan, ought to hang on the studio wall of every student. It is important — very important. Failure to appreciate the part that paper does play in the success — or failure — of any work of art is one of the greatest sources of discouragement. Repeatedly, in my field criticisms I have given no other direction than, "Get a piece of such and such paper and try that again." The result has sometimes seemed miraculous.

Take nothing for granted when selecting papers. Do not assume, for example, that "charcoal" paper is just what you want for a sketching in charcoal. Probably it is just what you should avoid. It is admirably suited for studies from the figure — and I dare say some find it suitable for landscape work — but I would never take it outdoors if I could get something else, almost anything else. The superiority of a sheet of cold-pressed watercolor paper is startling. On it, the soft vine charcoal gives a deep black of velvet quality. A gentle rub with a finger reduces the black to lovely grays. The kneaded eraser, shaped between thumb and finger to a sharp edge, will pick out pure white streaks as keen as a knife cut. Or, if large areas need to be erased for correction, the kneaded eraser will wipe them clean, leaving the surface fresh, ready for further work.

Not everyone will agree with my choice of cold-pressed; others will find some other surface more congenial. The point is that there are innumerable papers and boards from which to choose; experiment with many until the surface best suited to *you* is discovered. Not that there is only *one* best. For different subjects and different kinds of treatment, various papers may be selected.

What I have said about papers for charcoal applies, of course, to papers for all mediums: pencil, watercolor, pastel or pen. Try every surface you can get your hands on. Use one paper one day, another the next. You will discover that some resist your efforts; others invite and actually cooperate in your creative purpose, responding eagerly to your every whim, even adding something — in the way they react to your medium — beyond your best expectation.

The beginner in art is prone to think that almost any material is good enough for his early essays, and the cheaper the better. He is likely to reason that in these early struggles he produces nothing worth *saving;* why should he waste good materials in transitory exercises? He overlooks the waste of his time and abilities in struggling with unresponsive equipment. Years ago I had the desire to play the mandolin. I bought the cheapest instrument I could find and took a few private lessons. I acquired a modicum of skill. One day I visited a friend who was an accomplished mandolin player. He suggested that we try a duet. After mud-dling through the selection he said, "Now let's exchange instruments." The response of my friend's excellent mandolin to my comparatively unskilled efforts gave me a thrill of pleasure. My own poor instrument had never produced music like that. It had never even met me halfway; it had actually resisted me.

Difficult as it is to do it, the beginner must learn to overcome the fear of spoiling a sheet of expensive paper. The best way to do this is to keep reminding himself that the inferior substitute probably will not cooperate with him and he will, in all truth, be losing both money and time in the practice of economy. One student had, I thought, an ingenious method. He bought ten dollars' worth of his favorite watercolor paper, believing that if he had a big stack of it instead of a few preciously hoarded sheets he might think less of its cost. He said the subterfuge worked.

I've sketched more with pencil than with any other medium and I am very fussy about paper. I worked for years on a lovely sheet which I had discovered after long experimentation with different papers. Finally the paper went off the market and I had to search for another surface. I found the surface, but its color was a cold white. Although it *felt* all right and actually produced excellent technical results, I couldn't do my best work on it because its color repelled me. I had to search further for a paper with an inviting warmth of color.

It is not my purpose here to catalog specific papers for different mediums. This is a highly personal matter and it would be futile to go further than to hint at approximate qualities to look for. Everyone, as I have said, must solve his own problems by trial and error. Again I say, "Try a dozen or more papers before believing you have found the best."

In testing papers we have to consider not only how the different surfaces receive the pencil or other mediums but how susceptible they are to erasure. Some papers are wholly prejudiced against erasers; others are friendly to them.

In pencil drawing it is advisable to have several sheets between the drawing and the drawing board. This yielding surface is much more agreeable than the hard surface of the board when the leads bear down upon the paper.

When it comes to drawing *for reproduction*, choice of paper is especially important; a cold white paper is preferable to cream or ivory. Any trace of yellow will be translated into gray tone by the photoengraving process. Even a cold white paper reproduces as light gray (called "screen") in the halftone process, as will be seen in the drawings on pages 34 and 35. The engraver can remove this screen by the highlight halftone process (see the drawing on page 19) but this is a very expensive process. Such reproductions cost approximately three times as much as regular halftones.

This little pattern sketch for my pencil drawing of St. Germain in France was done in a minute or two, before beginning the drawing. In it I organized my design, planning the values and simplifying the tonal scheme. It is fairly close to the actual effect, as I recall.

In addition to the darkest shadow tone which is really the basic compositional motive, I planned for only two other tones, a very light one on the faces of the two buildings and an intermediate one on the roofs. It will be seen that I followed this pattern scheme rather faithfully in the final drawing.

In this thumbnail sketch I was doing precisely what I have recommended (on the first pages) doing with brush and ink. My purpose in urging the brush experiments was to help in acquiring a habit of analytical thinking that would apply in a situation of this kind.

Practically every subject calls for this sort of planning, without which a sketch is likely to be confusing.

In starting a sketch I almost always lay-in the darkest tones first. In the St. Germain subject I began with the black notes under the awnings, then rendered the dark shaded sides of the buildings and the cast shadow. Probably the roofs came next, then the lightest tones. Last of all, the clouds and the lines of the curb.

The clouds and the lightest notes at the edges are responsible for the vignetting of the sketch. This again is a matter of design. How to "get out" of a drawing is almost as difficult for a beginner as getting into it. The vignette has to be considered not only as design but as illustration. It must be so artfully handled that the spectator doesn't think about it at all. Yet it ought to suggest a continuation of the scene in every direction.

SKETCH BY THE AUTHOR IN ST. GERMAIN, FRANCE

Courtesy Joseph Dixon Crucible Co.

Unless one wishes to copy the tonal effect of this subject as seen in the snapshot, it is necessary to plan an arbitrary pattern of dark and light that focuses attention upon areas of the structure that one deems especially interesting. Here we have a quite different situation than the St. Germain street scene where the color areas and shadows gave us something more tangible to work with in the way of pattern.

In the pencil drawing I have created what might be called a "path of interest" traveling along the shadowed lower story and up the face of the structure diagonally. That is only one of several possible schemes.

The diagrammatic pen sketch above focuses attention in about the same areas, but does it by surrounding them with dark instead of making them dark. Focus of interest, it thus appears, can be produced either by a dark spot surrounded by light, or vice versa.

The original pencil sketch — the same size as the reproduction — was made on a sunny day, as my snapshot shows. It was done with three or four leads of varying degrees. That accounts for the very smooth quality of light tones which if rendered with the same soft leads needed for dark tones would have a grained and coarse aspect.

SKETCH OF THE THEATRE OF MARCELLUS
BY THE AUTHOR

Courtesy Joseph Dixon Crucible Co.

25

1

2

3

4

A Problem
In Composition

The Italian street scene pictured in the snapshot above (Piazza Granda Fontana, Assisi) presents a problem in composition that is familiar to all artists who make a practice of sketching on the spot.

If the shadow shapes and values in this subject are copied literally, the sketch will be as confusing as the photograph. Shadows on the fountain and those on buildings beyond are of approximately the same value. They create a confusing pattern in which the form and character of the fountain are lost (figure 1).

The fountain obviously is the center of interest; and its environment, though important, is of quite secondary interest. By making a dark silhouette of the fountain (figure 2) we realize its structural unity. By lightening the shadows of the background we establish a proper sense of distance — give a feeling of the space that separates foreground and background. Figure 3 represents an experiment designed to give more unity to the composition through the disposition of tone and shadow in the distance. In figure 4 we see another trial which is more promising. This plan, it will be seen, makes for better legibility than the design of figure 3, because the fountain is given a light background against which it is massed as a dark unit — the scheme of figure 2. This is the plan followed in the final pencil drawing.

Note that the roofs in my drawing have been made darker than in the photo, and the shadow on the right side of the building is quite dark near the roof, although it fades to a very light tone below to favor the silhouetting of the fountain mass. The modified shape of this shadow serves to tie together the fountain mass

SKETCH OF PIAZZA GRANDA FONTANA, IN ASSISI, ITALY

and the roofs; these are disconnected in the photo. A slight change in roof structure serves to give a more interesting silhouette at the skyline. In the photo the roof contours flow into one another in a too-smooth horizontal line.

It is seldom that one finds a composition "ready-made," and the artist should feel free to take such liberties with facts as will add to the dramatic effect of his drawing. Slight alterations in details, even changes in proportions and the relative positions of buildings and objects are unimportant in an illustrative sense, yet they may make the difference between good and bad composition. For example, the fountain in my sketch might have been moved considerably to the right (had it seemed desirable) without violating the memory of those quite familiar with the scene.

The original drawing for the pencil study was done on Warren's Cameo, the paper referred to on page 13.

A soft lead gives rich, velvet-like tones on this paper, both in the dark and light values, and a delightful quality is imparted to the drawing. Cameo comes in several different weights. The heaviest is called "postcard" stock and that is what I recommend for sketching. Its thick coating of clay is a great advantage, especially if you want to use the razor blade on it.

Erasers are not effective on Cameo. They just smudge the tones. A sharp razor blade can be used instead. But the blade is much more than a substitute for the eraser; it is employed to pick out clean white accents from pencil tones. No matter how dark and solid the tones, a light touch or scrape with the blade (it must be very sharp) will expose the white paper underneath and give your sketch life and sparkle.

Another of my favorite papers is Strathmore "Alexis," a rather smooth surface — though having a very agreeable tooth. I seldom use rough surfaces for pencil. A plate-finished bristol board is also excellent when drawing with soft leads.

Smooth papers require soft leads; rougher surfaces will take harder leads.

27

Clarity
Out of Confusion

One spring morning while wandering with my camera in New York's lower East Side, I came upon the scene shown above. I got it on a film, thinking I might have some use for the horses and wagon. When I saw the print it seemed to be a good subject to use in this book in connection with our discussion of pattern in sketching.

Just what might one do with such a confusing subject? For one thing, the team and wagon ought to be made legible. That would mean silhouetting them against a background of contrasting value, bringing them out from the confusion behind them. The sacks of paper stock on the wagon are already massed against the dark shadow — but the horses, being the same value as the buildings behind them, are lost. We could turn them into white horses — the off horse is actually white — but it will serve our purpose better to keep them dark and lighten the background. This will fit in with our need for a simpler pattern scheme as expressed in the diagram below the photograph. In this we retain the dark foil for the light wagon and give the horses the setting they need.

The lower diagram shows further development of the composition. Intermediate tones and details embellish but do not alter the basic pattern. The two factory chimneys in the distance are improvised in order to prevent the interest sliding off at the left along the sloping roof lines. They also give a spot of dark which is needed here as a matter of balance. Cover them with a piece of paper and you will see how important they are.

Use
Your Imagination

The photograph of the horse and wagon was taken late of a market day in Wallabout Market, Brooklyn. Two or three hours earlier the scene would have appeared more as shown in one of the two composition studies under the picture. Both show obvious means for getting pattern interest as well as illustrative activity. This kind of experimentation is the artist's habitual practice in dramatizing subjects that call for the exercise of his imagination.

Note how the silhouetting of horse and wagon varies in accordance with changes in background treatment — light against dark; dark against light.

The student might like to develop this subject further in a sketch. I suggest making a vignette of it. This involves some improvisation since the character of the building is not revealed in the photograph. It might be interesting to substitute a black horse and see how that would affect the background and the composition as a whole.

Almost everything the artist does makes demands upon imagination. The more of *that* he has, the more of an artist he is. Without it he is no more than a copyist, holding the conviction that accurate reporting is what is desired of him most of all. There is no better way to encourage development of this power than to experiment with the composition of your subjects, rearranging, substituting, trying every device you can think of for their most dramatic presentation. No one knows or cares what your subject looked like; what you make of it is all that counts.

29

How About Size?

One of the first decisions an artist must make concerns size. How large shall he plan his sketch or his painting? The way he answers the question is important. It may mean the difference between success and failure; at least it will qualify his success. There is *just the right size* for his work, whatever it may be.

There are many factors to be considered. One is time. It would be folly for the painter to take along a large canvas when for one reason or another — rapidly changing light, for example — he will have not over an hour for his sketch. The inconvenience of a large canvas on a windy day or in a busy thoroughfare is another factor. The necessity for quickly recording some moving action, such as haymaking, is still another. Most painters confine their outdoor sketching to small panels that fit in their paint boxes, or to relatively small papers if they are working in watercolor.

But aside from these contingent factors there are others, inherent in the various mediums, which impose definite limitations. It is technically possible to make a pen sketch 20 x 30 inches but no one would think of doing it. A 20 x 30 inch canvas, on the other hand, presents a relatively small scale for a painter in oils, a medium that can manage a 20 x 30 foot mural gracefully. Watercolors are kept within narrower space limits, as are pastels. The pencil — though, like the pen, a point medium — when handled broadly will produce a stroke many times as broad as a pen line. However it is not a medium for large-scale work. Architects, to be sure, do make pencil renderings four or five feet long to visualize proposed buildings for their clients. But as we are discussing sketching, we are not concerned with these elaborate drawings intended to illustrate details and suggest textures of building materials, as well as to give an impression of the whole design.

Do not make your pencil drawings too large.

What is *too* large? The answer depends somewhat upon the subject. A castle or a skyscraper may suggest a larger drawing than a boathouse, but an 8 x 10 inch pencil drawing of a castle is certainly as large as I would attempt. I practically never work larger than that, and my preference is for an even smaller scale. The largest sketch of the boathouse on the opposite page is reproduced at exact size of my original. For beginners I strongly recommend very small drawings; they will thus escape the danger of becoming hypnotized by detail.

Charcoal is a mass medium. It is more closely related to pastel than to pencil and can handle a 16 x 20 or larger size very easily. It produces textural qualities that give interest to relatively large unbroken areas, such as the left side of the boathouse, that in a sizeable drawing would be very difficult for the pencil or pen. But charcoal cannot compete — in the matter of size — with pastel or the painting mediums that have color as well as texture to offer.

It is by way of illustrating some of these size factors that I have made the six drawings of the boathouse originally sketched on the Cornish Coast of England. They are here reproduced at exact size and are intended to suggest how the structure might be rendered when seen at varying distances.

The largest is obviously a close-up. It is, as I have said, as big as I would care to sketch it in pencil and it has all the detail afforded by the subject. To draw it larger would force the pictorial details at the expense of general effect.

The smallest sketch is about the way the structure might appear at a distance of, say, a quarter of a mile.

Light and shadow, seen at a distance, show a limited range of values: there are no very dark tones. As we come nearer, the darks appear and, when close, we see the complete tonal gamut.

But it is well to keep in mind the simplified light and dark pattern of that far-distant effect when working on our close-ups; not to do so is to run the risk of losing clarity and sense of volume. In larger drawings it is very easy to become so diverted by illustrative detail that the big pattern — hence compositional power — is sacrificed. It is fairly common practice among artists to preface their final drawings or paintings with thumbnail sketches which help them to see their subjects in simple and effective patterns.

Large drawings simply demand detail. There should be no inactive areas. Every part of the picture must have something to say. When a large area is devoid of illustrative interest the drawing fails to convince; it looks empty. In this connection, refer to the various treatments of the boathouse roof. In the first four sketches the roof is so small that the textural interest of the pencil strokes themselves satisfies the need for detail.

In the fifth drawing we begin to feel the need for greater interest in the roof and in the largest one it was necessary to give a definite impression of an ancient patched roof that probably leaks during heavy rains. The roof of sketch 5 would look unfinished if duplicated in sketch 6.

It is safe to say that most beginners get into a lot of trouble by working too large in any medium. They set themselves tasks that would worry even practiced artists. In large scale it is so difficult to get what we call "quality." Of course other factors than size enter into that: such things as the right paper and proper grade of pencil, to mention two.

I should remind the reader that the foregoing remarks about size apply only to drawings that have no other purpose beyond their own charm. Painters, accustomed to large-scale work with the brush, often make sizeable pencil notes purely as records or as studies for paintings. They do this with no thought of producing drawings to delight the eye.

There is still another factor that must be considered in our discussion of size. That is the artist's own temperament. Some people naturally do their best work at small scale, others can function only at larger size. "Large-scale" people usually write with a bold, scrawling hand. They like to draw with arm movement rather than finger movement. These individual, temperamental qualities ought to be considered; they are important. The large-scale person probably will never be as effective with pen and pencil as with charcoal, pastel or painting mediums. This is something each individual must discover and act accordingly.

Happy Accidents

The other day I sat down on a New England stone wall to sketch a group of old oaks under which a herd of cows had sought shelter from the summer sun. The drawing started out all right but it didn't go well. That sometimes happens, you know!

Finally, I lost interest in it and gave it up, slipped my failure into my portfolio and just sat basking in the peace of the rural scene. But not for long. I really wanted to record the *spirit* of those old trees — so I reached for paper and pencil once more. I decided not to try to copy the form of any single tree but to *design* one that would express the character of several veterans that were putting up a last brave fight.

With a very soft graphite pencil I began playing around with foliage masses, somewhat in the manner of the top sketch on the page opposite. Holding the pencil between thumb and forefinger and in the palm of my hand — much as one holds a charcoal stick — I lightly scumbled in a foliage mass, trying to design as I went along, but without any preconceived notion of just how my tree would finally develop. I wasn't even looking at the trees in the meadow; I was concentrating wholly upon my own creation.

Finally, within the penciled mass, accidental lines and spottings began to suggest things and with little effort on my part, seemingly, the tree began to take shape. It grew into what you see above.

I am confessing, you see, that *accident*, the accident of those pencil scumblings, is responsible for my tree. Well, not quite, perhaps, for one must concede that better accidents happen when practiced hands hold the pencil. That is not all: only an artist will recognize happy accidents and have the ability to take advantage of them.

What I am getting at is the undeniable fact that accidents are useful. Every artist will admit it. Few good pictures, it is safe to say, come to final perfection without the aid of innumerable technical accidents which the artist has been resourceful enough to exploit. Whatever the medium — oil, watercolor, pastel, tempera, pencil, charcoal, or ink — such accidents are bound to happen. But they are more prone to happen with one medium than another. Perhaps they are less likely to happen with pen and ink than with any other medium. Charcoal will do a lot for you in the way of accidents. Experiment with various mediums with this in mind.

The diagrams on the opposite page will suggest, I think, how the pencil — soft lead on a roughish paper — will produce happy accidents when it is handled in the manner of charcoal with the broad side of the lead. The several pages following will demonstrate how generously charcoal cooperates with the artist in this respect.

A SUBJECT RENDERED WITH SEVERAL PENCILS

Again, on the page opposite, we see a drawing rendered with a very soft lead pencil. Here the tortillon stump was employed to smudge the pencil tones in places. But note that it was used sparingly. The grained texture of the unrubbed pencil tones is quite expressive of stone quality and the sketch would have suffered from a too general use of the stump.

The function of the stump and the kneaded eraser in a pencil sketch is the same as when used with charcoal. The swatch of tone at the top of the opposite plate clearly demonstrates this. The eraser has been kneaded to a sharp edge to take out those thin white lines.

Below the finished drawing I have shown approximately how the sketch started. It shows how accidental effects suggest structure and detail as described on the preceding pages. Naturally, these accidents are subordinate to the facts of the subject which are consciously portrayed. It is in the incidents rather

than the basic structure that we expect technical accidents to control our pencil.

The above drawing of the same subject was made afterward in order to offer comparison between the soft pencil technique on page 35 and a rendering with several grades of lead. Four leads were employed to produce the tones represented by the swatches 1, 2, 3 and 4. The lightest tone is the work of a rather hard lead, perhaps an H. The darkest tone (4) was obtained with a 3B or 4B. The intermediate tones 2 and 3 probably indicate B and 2B, respectively. The degree of lead required for a given tone depends much upon the humidity of the atmosphere; the dryer the air, the harder the leads needed.

At 5 we see the kind of point used in applying the strokes. The lead is first sharpened as if for writing, then worn down on a piece of scrap paper until it produces fairly wide strokes.

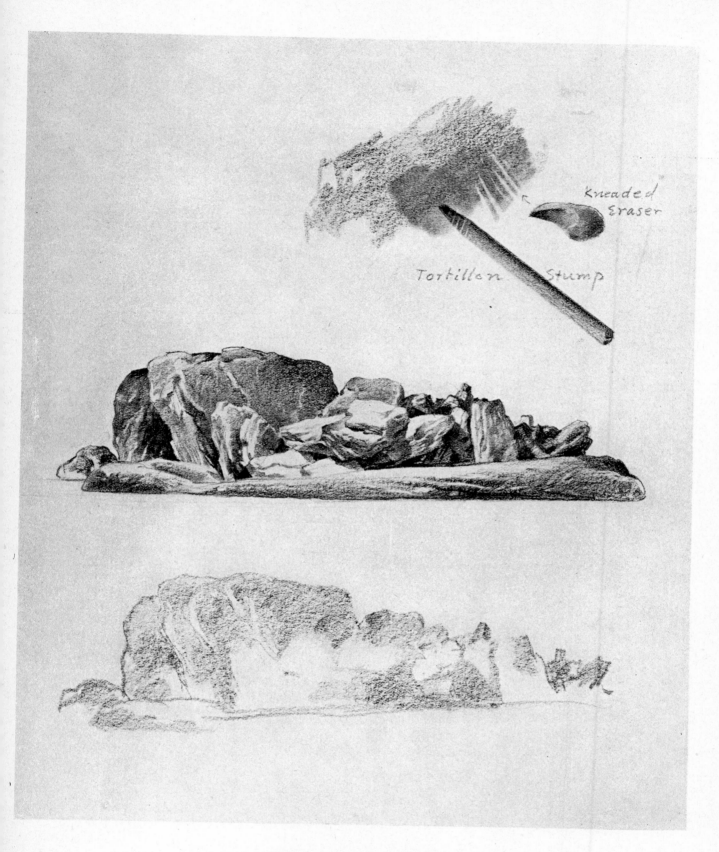

Kneaded Eraser

Tortillon Stump

DEMONSTRATING THE TECHNIQUE
OF SOFT LEAD PENCIL AND TORTILLON STUMP

Charcoal

I have already had something to say about charcoal in my chapters on *Paper* and *Happy Accidents*. Although in my opinion this is one of the most felicitous of all sketching mediums, for some reason it is not very popular. I want to recommend it to students and to artists who may not have discovered its possibilities.

Charcoal may be had in hard, medium and soft sticks. The hard and medium varieties are the best known, as they are commonly employed in drawing from the figure in school art classes. For this purpose charcoal is used principally as a point medium and it works best on charcoal paper.

The soft variety is better for sketching, and in the following discussion about charcoal this is the type referred to. In the drawings themselves this is the medium employed. It is known as *vine* charcoal and it comes in thin sticks a trifle larger than (3) in the accompanying plate. The sticks break easily but that is no disadvantage; I usually break them at the outset into pieces two or three inches long, or even one inch long as in (1) and (2), shown with the swatches of tone produced by these short lengths.

The sketches that follow demonstrate some of the possibilities of this eagerly responsive medium and the diagrams on the facing page give a hint as to how these effects are obtained.

That very short stick, scumbled broadside on a proper surface, will render tones that are indeed full of happy accidents. It produces tones of great textural charm. When rubbed with the finger as in (4) the character is entirely different. The tortillon stump (5) renders quite another kind of tone (not too evident in the reproduction). The kneaded eraser (6), shaped between the thumb and finger to a knife-like edge, will take thin white strokes out of a dark mass, and of course will remove larger areas as desired. The thin strokes at (7) are made, not by pointing the stick but by using the edge of the round end. Of course a hard stick, pointed, will do this too.

Now all these effects can be combined in a single drawing if desired. They are readily identified in the accompanying examples. Just when to rub a tone and when to leave the scumble untouched by finger or stump is one of those subtle decisions that make or mar the sketch. Generally speaking, it is wise to rub sparingly. Excessive smudging of the tones is likely to give a labored effect.

In the *Paper* chapter I have already made some suggestions about surfaces that are receptive to charcoal. Let me repeat here that everyone should search, by experiment, for the paper that suits the individual taste. Some papers refuse to register the velvet-black tones which charcoal will produce on just the right surface. Other papers will take the black all right but will hold it so permanently that the eraser is helpless. Just the right paper will receive the black and give it up freely when touched with the kneaded eraser. A soft paper is not likely to serve at all. Watercolor papers are promising. Illustration board is excellent. Even some varieties of tracing paper will do nicely.

Kneaded erasers come in rectangular cakes. Tear or cut off a piece the size of a marble and knead with the fingers until soft and pliable. The rubber then can be moulded to a point or to the thin edge recommended for such uses as will be seen in the drawings here reproduced. After the eraser has absorbed about so much charcoal it should be discarded, as when dirty it will leave dark smears on the paper.

Charcoal drawings require spraying with fixative to prevent rubbing. The spray pipes sold in the stores will do, but they take a lot of lung power and it is difficult not to inhale the poisonous vapor. A spray gun such as is used for spraying Flit is better.

Avoid too much fixative. An excess amount will stain the drawing yellow. Spray a little at a time, then test the black parts with the finger.

You will probably work on a larger scale with charcoal than with pencil. However, as stated in the chapter on *Size*, the temperamental factor counts a lot. If you do better when working on a small scale you need not make large sketches in charcoal; you will soon learn to manage this medium in very small sizes. On the other hand, if you like to fling your arms about, you will have a wonderful time with charcoal on a 16 x 20 paper.

2

3

4

5

6

7

kneaded
eraser

CHARCOAL SKETCH BY THE AUTHOR

One-half size of original

CHARCOAL SKETCH BY THE AUTHOR

Drawn in studio after the sketch on page 39, which was done in the field. Note the various effects due to different ways of handling the medium. The blacks represent the full strength of the soft charcoal. Light grays, scumbled on with an unsharpened stick, give the medium tones which here and there were touched with the tortillon stump. The lowest light branch which rests on the ground shows some rendering with a sharply pointed stick. The kneaded eraser was employed for the white trunk and branches, as well as for white lights on the foliage masses.

41

CHARCOAL STUDY BY THE AUTHOR

One-half size of original

CHARCOAL DRAWING BY THE AUTHOR

The original study, drawn on the spot, on a summer afternoon, is about 20 x 24 inches. Compare the meticulous rendering of this subject with the preceding hastily done sketches.

Quill Pen
A Drawing Tool of The Old Masters

Here and there in this book I have spoken of materials and tools which might be expected to "cooperate" with the artist in his creative experiences. I have called attention, for example, to the way charcoal and pencil can be induced actually to suggest effects which might not have been a part of the artist's intention. I have emphasized the urgency for the artist to discover those tools which best respond to his temperament. I made the statement that of all drawing tools the pen is perhaps the most "uncooperative." Of course I referred to the steel pen which is quite rigid and, as I said, will only do what it is *forced* to do. Perhaps this statement will be refuted by expert penmen who have learned how to get the utmost out of this inflexible tool, but I am thinking now of those who may be taking up their pens for the first time.

The old masters habitually employed a drawing tool that is vastly superior to our modern steel pens which, of course, were unknown to them. That was the pen made from turkey or goose feathers. It produces a line that responds sympathetically to the artist's impulse. It is flexible, ranging from hair-line delicacy to bold, broad accents that are almost brush-like in effect.

The quill gives solid blacks and beautiful gradations of tone to light grays, depending upon how it is used. It is smooth; the quill glides over the paper without effort. The quill pen, as we are reminded by William Palmer, who employs it, will not tear the paper, as do sharp steel pens. Quills from the wings are the largest, and they are more nearly round; they are preferred to the flatter tail feathers. The old masters used crow quills for very fine work. This is the origin of the name now given to extra-fine steel pens.

The diagram on the page following gives explicit directions for making these pens.

There is nothing difficult about this procedure, but it may take a bit of experimenting before you can produce just the kind of a point you prefer. For one thing you will need a *very* sharp knife in making the cuts. The razor blade can only be used at stages 2 and 6; the curved cuts require a narrow blade.

To keep the quills in good condition they must be kept moist; stand them in a jar of water and they will last quite a long time, retaining their resiliency and their working points.

Many of the old master drawings were executed in a brown ink and were heightened with a wash of *bistre*, a brownish watercolor made from the soot of burned wood. That is the technique of the Rembrandt drawing shown on the page opposite.

A considerable variety of effect can be obtained through experimentation with various inks. When a waterproof ink is used, the line is not affected by a wash laid down over it. Other inks, of course, will be picked up by the wet brush to the extent of the moisture and the manner in which the brush is handled. The degree of dryness of the ink line is also a factor; if the line is allowed to dry thoroughly before the wash is applied, there will be less drag.

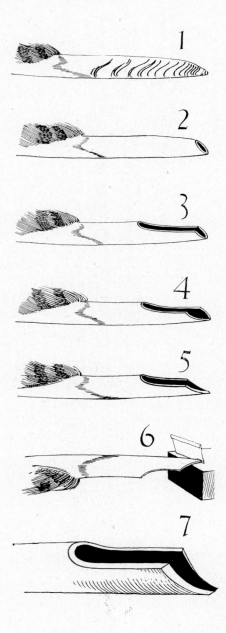

Artists often prefer the regular inks *because* they respond to the wash by blurring and otherwise merging here and there in the watercolor mass. Indeed, many of the handsomest drawings in this medium rely to a considerable extent upon the "marriage" of pen line and brush wash. The student will experience much delight in these possibilities.

Don't overlook, here, the possibilities in papers. As in most others mediums, paper is fully as important as the drawing tool itself. It is known that some of the much admired sketches by old masters were done on blank pages of old books printed on handmade papers. A fine rag-content sheet certainly has properties not found in most commercial papers.

Watercolor papers are especially recommended when wash is to be combined with the quill; not the very rough surfaces, to be sure. The very smooth bristols made for pen drawing are very unsympathetic to this medium; they are cold and hard. Many artists prefer their lines to be less sharply defined. They like to have their rigidity modified by rougher surfaced papers that will give "quality" to the rendering.

Now for an explanation of the diagram.

Figure 1 shows the uncut quill and its fibrous structure within. After the first cut has been made (2) these fibres can be removed easily, leaving the quill ready for the next cut. Make this cut (3) not with a single stroke of the knife, but with two: one for each side of the quill. Hold the blade so that it cuts a bevel away from the center of the quill. Fig. 4 shows one side of the point cut back as a first step in bringing the quill to a proper point. In fig. 5 the other side has been cut. These two cuts are made on a bevel as described in fig. 3 and shown more clearly in fig. 7. At fig. 6 we see a razor blade or sharp knife cutting across the point, trimming it to a straight edge. This may be as narrow or wide as desired: the narrower it is, the finer the line produced. Note that this last cut is also made on a bevel so as to produce a chisel-like point.

We are indebted to Dean Fawcett for these directions for the preparation of quills, for the diagrams, and for the photograph on the preceding page. Fawcett has made many handsome drawings with this medium. Study of the drawings by Delacroix and Rembrandt will demonstrate the possibilities of the quill pen. Note how each master varies his line from hair-line delicacy to very broad, bold strokes.

Fragment of a quill drawing by Delacroix, that demonstrates the flexible and fluid quality of this tool.

A QUILL PEN DRAWING BY REMBRANDT

This is typical of innumerable landscape sketches by the master, done with quill pen and bistre wash. Bistre is a watercolor made from the soot of burned wood. It has a pleasant sepia color. Courtesy Metropolitan Museum of Art.

Color Drawings

The introduction of color into a black and white sketch opens up fascinating possibilities to the student of outdoor sketching.

What, one might inquire, in examining the illustrations shown in this book, is the difference between a color drawing and a painting? Turning from my drawing of *Deserted House*, on page 51, to Louis C. Rosenberg's *Copenhagen Fish Market*, on page 57, to my *Jumbled Buildings* (frontispiece), to William C. Palmer's drawing, on page 65, to Henry Varnum Poor's drawing, on page 93, and finally to my pastel, on page 53, the question seems justified.

The answer would seem to reside in the artist's *intention*, rather than in the actual result. When he applied his color, was he drawing or was he painting? These are two different attitudes. It is not easy to define the distinction, because at times the attitudes are so correlated or integrated that even the artist himself may not be able to say when he is drawing and when he is painting. However, when he is trying to express color, or texture, or other qualities definitely associated with painting, the distinction is clear. William C. Palmer makes an interesting contribution to the discussion in the following comment he has made upon the purpose and function of his own drawings — in color and in black and white. The kind of drawing he refers to, it will be seen, relates specifically to his painting; it is drawing as a means to an end rather than drawing for its own sake.

"Drawing, I believe," says Mr. Palmer, "is one of the most important tools at the command of the artist. In his tools he discovers the most personal expressions, aims, and attitudes of the creative personality. I make hundreds of drawings, for in them I express my experiences and emotions freely. Since I am a painter, I had to discover a method which would give me the same pleasure as painting, and at the same time allow for experimentation. The assurance and permanence of ink and the security in the line prompted this method for gathering information. I have never set out to produce a drawing without having been moved by some notion for a painting, or to make a record of an experience. All of my works are produced from memory which is aided by the small notes I make with my fountain pen on the backs of envelopes or on small pieces of paper which I carry in my pocket.

"Since creating a design is to me a great personal experience, I have come to depend upon my drawings to encourage and stimulate my work. Usually some notion or problem forces me to draw, and in drawing I express my limitations as well as my understanding. For me to have a complete realization of what the drawing is to look like before I start would end in my not doing it at all. In the drawing one states all he knows. The rhythms, balance, pattern and unity are expressed with economy, assurance and validity. One cannot set out to produce a work of art, but one can set out to work out a problem. That is why I use drawing and its freeing element to investigate and express ideas and experiences.

"It is encouraging to me to see that this art form (drawing) is being exploited, and that more and more large exhibitions of both old and modern masters are being held. At no time in the great periods of art has this medium been neglected. And to discover the base upon which the masters produced their work one has only to go to their sketches and drawings to learn of their problems, most intimate thoughts, and experiments. Drawing is fun; and if one is content to make numerous attempts for perhaps one successful result, then the world is at his command. Anything can be expressed in a drawing. A drawing a day, and at least most of them from memory, will in the end result in an invaluable collection of material for reference and stimulation."

Mr. Palmer's emphasis upon drawing from memory is interesting. Those who have not had this experience will discover that in its practice one acquires new powers, both of seeing and of expressing. When viewing a subject with the purpose of memorizing, one sharpens his faculty of observation, realizing that the mental image must be especially strong if it is to be retained.

A subject envisioned in memory ought also to result in a more significant statement because unessential details are likely to be sifted out, leaving its broader aspect in the mind. This is a bigger factor than the beginner is likely to appreciate.

A variety of mediums have been used in the color drawings here reproduced. One of the most common is pen and sepia watercolor. This gives effects like those seen in my *Deserted House* (page 51), and Rosenberg's *Copenhagen Fish Market* (page 57). Edmund Yaghjian's sketch on page 91 is in pen and gray wash. My frontispiece drawing, *Jumbled Buildings*, goes a step further toward painting technique in its use of a variety of diluted colors. Henry Varnum Poor's drawing (page 93) was executed in pastel and black ink applied with the brush. I have experimented with color on pencil drawings, but without much satisfaction; the pencil, unless used with great vigor, is too delicate to carry color or even gray washes. Carbon pencil or lithographic pencils can support color because they give black rather than gray tones.

Generally speaking, color is considered supplementary to line, being employed to enhance the line effect rather than to dominate it. But it is evident that both Mr. Poor and Mr. Palmer were thinking color rather than line. Between the two extremes there is a wide range of purpose and method in the use of color. Every artist will, of course, follow his own inclination and discover his own preferences, but the beginner might well be advised to try his luck at first with simple sepia or gray washes over his line drawings.

DESERTED HOUSE   PEN AND SEPIA SKETCH BY THE AUTHOR

This reproduction is reduced to about two-thirds the size of the original draw-
ing. The sketch was made on cold-pressed watercolor paper, with a fine pen
and a No. 5 sable brush. The house was first lightly sketched in with pencil.

PASTEL SKETCH BY THE AUTHOR

*The drawing was done with square pastel sticks on illustration board in about
one hour. Very few colors were used.*

A Gallery of Examples

The author is very grateful to the artists whose work appears on the following pages. Some are painters, some printmakers, others illustrators; all are artists of distinction whose drawings offer great educational value and inspiration. The examples represent a wide range of subject matter and technical treatment. Not all of them can be called "sketches"; some are preliminary studies for paintings and etchings, a fact which in no way lessens their value to the sketching student.

It will be interesting, in studying these drawings, to question the artists' intention in making them. The pencil notes by Roy Brown on page 81 quite obviously were made as preludes to paintings. Probably they are bits of nature redesigned for the painter's canvas, rather than literal transcripts of the landscape. Helen A. Loggie's drawing is a most meticulous study for an etching which followed the drawing in every detail. Emil Kosa's *Hop Kilns* is a sketch from nature made for its own sake, as are the drawings by Norman Kent, Sam Thal, and others.

The student who uses the drawings on these pages as subjects for his own experiments will find this section of the book especially instructive. For example, try rendering Miss Loggie's trees in the technique employed by Arthur L. Guptill. Render E. G. Eisenlohr's subject (page 67) as Lester Hornby (page 69) might have handled it. Interpret Walter Jack Duncan's pen drawing (page 87) in color inspired by Henry Varnum Poor's sketch (page 93). Convert Gifford Beal's pencil sketch (page 95) into a pen drawing.

The novice may want to literally copy these examples as a means of acquiring facility in various techniques. That procedure will be profitable, but the translation of the subjects into different graphic languages — as suggested above — is a creative exercise that reveals more of the artist's power than slavish copying.

COPENHAGEN FISH MARKET

PEN AND WASH DRAWING BY LOUIS C. ROSENBERG

Louis Rosenberg is a name of distinction in the two professions of Architecture and Graphic Arts. His architectural training and practice have given him both viewpoint and structural knowledge to invest his work with brilliance and authority. His sketches in the field, as well as his etchings, invariably exhibit his extraordinary skill. In this sketch, done with a sparkling pen line and a few deft washes of sepia, he reveals the possibilities of this effective technique.

ROAD TO HUERTGEN   BY OGDEN PLEISSNER

CHARCOAL PENCIL DRAWING
WITH WATERCOLOR WASHES

*This is one of many drawings made by the artist during the summer of 1945
when he was in Europe on assignment from Life as war correspondent.*

PENCIL DRAWING BY MENALKAS T. SELANDER

This is a most unusual pencil drawing. Mr. Selander has succeeded in securing a very wide range of values with this graphite medium. His darkest tones are as black as black ink. The contrast of heavy dark masses and light delicate tones gives an unusual dramatic effect. The reproduction is about one-half the size of the original sketch.

HOP KILNS, SACRAMENTO   PENCIL DRAWING BY EMIL J. KOSA, JR.

*Emil Kosa, one of our most accomplished painters, uses his lead pencil with
unusual vigor. He has a fine sense of design which gives his work sureness and
distinction. Note how Kosa achieves perfect legibility through clarity of light
and shadow pattern.*

A COLOR DRAWING BY WILLIAM C. PALMER

Mr. Palmer has very generously told us just how he proceeded in making this and similar drawings. His comments upon materials and methods of work are given below.

"Materials: *Chinese inks, stick form, brown, blue black; heavy Whatman watercolor paper, cold-pressed; chinese brushes, reed and quill pens; sharp knife and ink eraser. Waterproof ink also makes fine washes, and I use it as well as the ink sticks.*

"Method of work: *Soak paper well with water, and stretch. Grind inks and mix tones: one gray, one blue and one brown. Keep these tones in bottles. I begin with the gray wash and, while the paper is wet, float on the large pattern with a big brush, allowing accidents to stimulate the creative work. Next, I apply the blue wash and design the blue areas. Since the paper is still wet, these two tones (blue and gray) will mix and blend, adding interesting variations. The brown comes last, as the design is further developed. By this time the paper is drying and the tones are becoming more settled and darker. I now take reed and quill pens to delineate forms; these are not sharp like steel pens so will not tear the paper. I continue to employ the three color tones until the result is satisfactory. By overlaying one color on top of another, various harmonious and subtle shades develop. After the major design is completed, I continue with reed and quill pens to add solidity and reality. Very fine drawing can be achieved with these tools and, as the paper is damp, a certain unity between the wash and the linear drawing results. The reed and quill technique affords a pleasing contrast to the softness of the wash.*

"*Before I complete a drawing of this kind, I put it up on the wall of the studio and look at it until it seems to tell me what it needs. Due to the process, there is little if any pure white left. To achieve the brilliance of pure white, I employ a sharp knife and scratch out the white areas. To complete the drawing, I heighten the light parts, and increase the force of the darks with inks.*"

SELMA ON THE CIBOLO   PENCIL DRAWING BY E. G. EISENLOHR

In this tender, poetic drawing, we note a wholly different technical approach than that of any other artist represented in this book. Mr. Eisenlohr works with a sharpened point, handled much as the skilled etcher handles his etching needle.

OLD QUARRY BUILDINGS

L.G. Hornby '37.
Rockport.

OLD QUARRY BUILDINGS, ROCKPORT, MASS.   PENCIL SKETCH BY LESTER HORNBY

Lester Hornby handles his pencil in a broad, painter-like manner. He is a superb draftsman and he knows how to get the utmost expression from his medium. Obviously he uses a broad stroke and several degrees of leads to secure such a wide range of values.

LEANING HOUSE, QUEBEC CARBON PENCIL DRAWING BY NORMAN KENT

This drawing is notable for its discriminating analysis which picks out the salient features of the subject and records them with a few simple tones and telling lines. We may be reminded here of the exercises in "legibility," presented on the first pages of this book, wherein the tonal effects are expressed in a few flat areas of shadow values.

Willows —
Vermont

A PENCIL DRAWING BY ARTHUR L. GUPTILL

*He knew just what he wanted to do and he did it without fumbling. Just goes
to show what you can express — if you're up to it — with a single soft lead
pencil and a joyous heart. Light, color, atmosphere; they're all here, set down
spontaneously on a July day in Vermont. Reproduction is slightly reduced
from the original.*

GLOUCESTER WHARF PENCIL SKETCH BY SAM THAL

This vigorous sketch by a Boston sculptor exhibits a rare skill in composition,
and a fine sense of values. Mr. Thal has employed his pencil in such a way as
to give life and sparkle to this interesting waterfront subject.

PENCIL SKETCH BY THEODORE KAUTZKY

Theodore Kautzky is a skillful exponent of the broad stroke method of pencil rendering. In this drawing, "View Down Fifth Avenue from 59th Street, New York," he uses his pencil in much the same manner as a brush, laying-in the tones in a painter-like technique. Kautzky's book, "Pencil Broadsides," demonstrates this brilliant technique.

THE NUNNERY, CHICHEN ITZA   PENCIL SKETCH BY THE AUTHOR

There's a particular thrill in sketching things that are alive with mystery as is this ruined Mayan temple of Chichen Itza in Yucatan. In rendering every historic stone, one envisions the ancient masons at work on their scaffolds, skillfully laying course upon course and hewing out those bizarre, sculptured ornaments that symbolize their strange religion. The problem presented here was to compose within the exactly square area of the temple façade. To avoid monotony, the artist decided to concentrate dark tones at the top and right of the structure, leaving the lower left corner in an unfinished state. But to balance the weight of dark on the right, the splash of jungle foliage was added at the left and the door filled with rich black.

LANDSCAPE SKETCHES BY ROY BROWN

These are pages from the sketchbooks of one of America's most distinguished painters. Note how Brown has resolved the landscape into a few simple, flat values. This kind of analysis is characteristic of his canvases and watercolors.

UNK AND ES   PENCIL STUDY FOR AN ETCHING BY HELEN A. LOGGIE

This etching-like pencil drawing is a marvel of meticulous draftsmanship, and
a superb nature study. Miss Loggie's drawings customarily are made with
Wolff carbon pencils HB, B, 2B and occasionally 3B. The HB and B she keeps
very sharp; some of the 2B's and 3B's are sharpened flat — with thin edge for
heavy darks; others of these with sharp points.

PEN SKETCH BY CHARLES KEENE

Charles Keene was an English illustrator who worked in the middle nineteenth century. This drawing is noteworthy for its extreme technical economy. The artist has succeeded in suggesting much with very few lines.

PEN DRAWING BY WALTER JACK DUNCAN

Walter Jack Duncan was one of America's "old masters" of pen illustration. Before the day of halftone reproduction his work was in much demand by editors and publishers. His sketch of the old shipyard is as fine a landscape study as he ever did. It was rendered with a fine-pointed pen, yet it combines tonal massing with great delicacy. The original is slightly larger than this reproduction; like pencil, the pen is a tool that is at its best in small drawings.

PENCIL SKETCH BY STANLEY WOODWARD

Stanley Woodward, noted painter of marines and old New England houses, here shows himself master of broad stroke pencil technique. Note how the artist has retained a sense of structure in this dilapidated building by means of simple light and shade — which give legibility — and not too broken rendering of the lighted planes. The original was about twice the size of this reproduction.

SKETCH IN CROW QUILL PEN AND WASH BY EDMUND YAGHJIAN

Says Yaghjian: "This sketch (14 x 16 inches) was made in 1941 in West Cornwall, Connecticut. I wanted to make a painting of the bridge and, as always, I made a study first. I sketch either in pencil or pen and ink. If there is a great deal of detail in what I want to paint, I make several drawings from more than one angle, in order to know just what is happening all around my subject. I find the better I know my subject, the better I can interpret it. Some students and artists who fail in producing interesting pictures from sketches will find that they have not studied the location or the subject enough, and have begun to paint before they have the picture complete in their sketch or in their mind."

A COLOR DRAWING BY HENRY VARNUM POOR

This stimulating sketch was done in pastel and india ink, slightly larger than this reproduction. It was made for no other eyes than the painter's, since his studies anticipate paintings and are thus merely a means to an end. However, a gifted artist is pretty certain to create something beautiful in even his most incidental work, as Poor has done in this subject.

PENCIL SKETCH BY GIFFORD BEAL

This sketch, 12 x 16 inches, was done with a very soft pencil. It is characteristic of the spirited quality of this famous painter's work in all mediums. Like practically all of Beal's drawings, it was intended as a possible motive for a painting, rather than a finished product for exhibition. Note the sureness and authority that are expressed in every stroke of the pencil.

LANDSCAPE DRAWING BY THOMAS GAINSBOROUGH, ENGLISH (1727–1788)

The original lead pencil drawing is 11 x 8 inches.

THE MOOR, FALMOUTH   CARBON PENCIL & WASH DRAWING BY MUIRHEAD BONE

Courtesy Metropolitan Museum of Art

FARMYARD WITH DUCKS   BY JULES DUPRÉ, FRENCH (1811–1889)

Drawn with Charcoal and White Chalk on Charcoal Paper